kiwi fruit and mint sauce

6 medium (500g) kiwi fruit, peeled, chopped

2 tablespoons caster sugar

3 teaspoons chopped fresh mint leaves

1 tablespoon gin

Blend or process kiwi fruit until smooth; push through sieve. Stir in sugar, mint and gin, stir until sugar dissolves. Refrigerate until cold. Serve with mini meringues.
Per serve fat 0.2g; kJ 406

melba sauce

425g can sliced peaches in syrup

200g fresh or frozen raspberries

1/3 cup (75g) caster sugar

1 1/2 teaspoons cornflour

1 1/2 tablespoons peach liqueur

Drain peaches; reserve 1/2 cup (125ml) syrup. Blend or process peaches and berries until smooth; push through fine sieve, discard seeds. Pour peach mixture into medium pan, add sugar, stir over heat until sugar dissolves. Stir in blended cornflour and reserved syrup, stir over heat until sauce boils and thickens. Stir in liqueur. Serve warm or cold with ice-cream.
Per serve fat 0.2g; kJ 712

Clockwise from top left: kiwi fruit and mint sauce, melba sauce, brandied apricot sauce.

brandied apricot sauce

1/2 cup (75g) chopped dried apricots

1 1/4 cups (310ml) water

2 tablespoons caster sugar

1/4 teaspoon ground cinnamon

2 teaspoons brandy

Combine apricots, water, sugar and cinnamon in medium pan; simmer, covered, about 5 minutes or until apricots are soft, cool. Blend or process apricot mixture with brandy until smooth. Serve with pancakes or waffles.
Per serve fat 0g; kJ 322

4

fresh figs and
dates in saffron syrup

contents

British & North American Readers:
Please note that Australian cup and
spoon measurements are metric. A quick
conversion guide appears on page 63.
A glossary explaining unfamiliar terms
and ingredients begins on page 60.

2 fruit sauces

mango and lime sauce

2 medium (860g) mangoes, peeled, chopped

2½ tablespoons lime juice

1 tablespoon Amaretto

Blend or process mangoes, juice and liqueur until smooth. Serve with fruit salad or cheesecake.
Per serve fat 0.3g; kJ 444

passionfruit sauce

You will need about 8 passionfruit for this recipe.

⅔ cup (160ml) passionfruit pulp

¼ cup (55g) caster sugar

½ cup (125ml) water

2 teaspoons cornflour

1 tablespoon water, extra

Combine undrained passionfruit pulp, sugar and water in small pan, stir over heat until sugar dissolves. Stir in blended cornflour and extra water, stir over heat until sauce boils and thickens.

Clockwise from top left: strawberry sauce, mango and lime sauce, passionfruit sauce.

Strain sauce, return 3 teaspoons of seeds to sauce; discard remaining seeds. Serve cold with ice-cream or fruit salad.
Per serve fat 0.1g; kJ 320

strawberry sauce

500g strawberries

¼ cup (40g) icing sugar mixture

2 teaspoons Grand Marnier

Blend or process all ingredients until smooth; strain. Serve with lemon tart or passionfruit souffle.
Per serve fat 0.1g; kJ 296

¾ cup (180ml) water

1 cup (250ml) dry white wine

½ cup (110g) caster sugar

5cm piece orange rind

pinch saffron threads

1 cinnamon stick

12 medium (720g) fresh figs, halved

8 (185g) fresh dates, seeded

crisp biscuits

30g soft butter

¼ cup (55g) caster sugar

1 egg white

2½ tablespoons plain flour

cooking oil spray

Combine water, wine and sugar in medium pan, stir over heat, without boiling, until sugar dissolves. Add rind, saffron and cinnamon, bring to boil; simmer, uncovered, 15 minutes. Strain syrup; discard rind, saffron threads and cinnamon. Return syrup to same pan, add figs; boil, uncovered, about 3 minutes or until syrup is thickened slightly. Remove from heat, add dates, cover; cool. Serve with Crisp Biscuits.

Crisp Biscuits Beat butter, sugar and egg white in small bowl with electric mixer, on low speed, until mixture is smooth and changed in colour; stir in sifted flour. Spoon mixture into piping bag fitted with 5mm plain tube. Pipe 8cm lengths onto oven trays which have been coated with cooking oil spray; make biscuits slightly wider at both ends. Allow 6 biscuits per tray. Tap tray on bench to make biscuits spread slightly. Bake in hot oven about 5 minutes or until edges are browned. Lift onto wire racks to cool.

Per serve fat 7.6g; kJ 2221

passionfruit liqueur
souffles

You will need about 4 passionfruit for this recipe.

cooking oil spray

1 tablespoon caster sugar

2 egg yolks

1/3 cup (80ml) passionfruit pulp

2 tablespoons La Grande Passion liqueur or Grand Marnier

1/2 cup (80g) icing sugar mixture

4 egg whites

Coat four 3/4-cup (180ml) ovenproof dishes with cooking oil spray. Sprinkle bases and sides with caster sugar; shake off excess. Place dishes on oven tray.

Whisk egg yolks, passionfruit, liqueur and 2 tablespoons of the icing sugar in medium bowl until combined. Beat egg whites in small bowl with electric mixer until soft peaks form; add remaining icing sugar, continue beating until firm peaks form.

Fold about a quarter of the egg white mixture into passionfruit mixture, then fold in remaining egg white mixture. Spoon into prepared dishes, bake in moderately hot oven about 12 minutes or until souffles are puffed. Serve immediately; dusted with a little sifted icing sugar and fresh fruit if desired.

Per serve fat 3.6g; kJ 794

mango, apple and passionfruit sorbet

You will need about 6 passionfruit for this recipe.

½ cup (110g) caster sugar

2 cups (500ml) apple juice

½ cup (125ml) water

425g can sliced mango in light syrup, drained

½ cup (125ml) passionfruit pulp

4 egg whites

Combine sugar, juice and water in medium pan, stir over heat, without boiling, until sugar dissolves. Bring to boil; simmer, uncovered, without stirring, about 12 minutes or until syrup is thickened slightly (syrup must not change colour), cool.

Blend or process mango until smooth. Stir mango and passionfruit into sugar syrup; pour into 20 x 30cm lamington pan. Cover with foil, freeze until just firm.

Beat sorbet mixture in small bowl with electric mixer until thick and fluffy. Return to pan, cover, freeze until just firm. Repeat beating process in large bowl, add egg whites 1 at a time, beat until fluffy. Return mixture to pan, cover, freeze until firm.

Per serve fat 0.1g; kJ 1130

lemon, lime and bitters

crush

2 cups (440g) caster sugar

2 cups (500ml) dry white wine

2 cups (500ml) water

1¹/₂ cups (375ml) lemon juice

¹/₂ cup (125ml) lime juice

1 teaspoon Angostura Aromatic Bitters

3 egg whites

Combine sugar, wine and water in large heavy-based pan, stir over heat, without boiling, until sugar dissolves. Bring to boil; simmer, uncovered, without stirring, about 20 minutes, or until syrup is thickened slightly (syrup must not change colour), cool to room temperature. Stir in juices and bitters. Pour mixture into 23cm square cake pan, cover with foil, freeze until firm.

Beat lemon mixture in large bowl with electric mixer until smooth. Beat egg whites in small bowl with electric mixer until firm peaks form; fold egg whites into lemon mixture in 2 batches. Return mixture to pan, cover, freeze until firm.

Per serve fat 0g; kJ2205

10 meringue-topped
plums

2 x 825g cans dark plums in syrup

¼ cup (60ml) sweet white wine

2 teaspoons lemon juice

1 tablespoon brown sugar

2 teaspoons cornflour

1 tablespoon water

2 egg whites

½ cup (110g) caster sugar

Drain plums, remove stones; reserve syrup. Combine reserved syrup, wine, juice and brown sugar in medium pan, bring to boil; simmer, uncovered, until reduced by half. Stir in blended cornflour and water, stir over heat until mixture boils and thickens.

Arrange plums in four 1-cup (250ml) shallow ovenproof dishes; pour syrup mixture over plums. Beat egg whites in small bowl with electric mixer until soft peaks form.

Add caster sugar gradually, beating until dissolved between additions. Spoon or pipe meringue mixture over plums in dishes. Bake, uncovered, in moderately hot oven about 5 minutes or until meringue is browned lightly.

Per serve fat 0.4g; kJ 2037

apple brown betty

cooking oil spray

2 cups (140g) stale breadcrumbs

4 large (800g) apples

1 teaspoon finely grated lemon rind

lemon syrup

½ cup (125ml) golden syrup

¼ cup (60ml) water

½ cup (110g) caster sugar

¼ cup (60ml) lemon juice

Coat 1.5-litre (6-cup) shallow ovenproof dish with cooking oil spray, sprinkle with a layer of breadcrumbs. Peel, core and grate apples coarsely, combine with rind in bowl.

Spread a layer of apple mixture over breadcrumbs. Repeat layering, finishing with breadcrumbs.

Pour hot Lemon Syrup over apple and bread mixture. Bake, uncovered, in slow oven about 1¼ hours or until lightly browned. Serve warm with low-fat yogurt, if desired.

Lemon Syrup Combine golden syrup, water and sugar in medium pan, stir over heat, without boiling, until sugar dissolves, remove from heat; stir in juice.

Per serve fat 1.8g; kJ 1729

12 petite summer
puddings

125g blackberries

200g raspberries

125g blueberries

250g strawberries, quartered

1/3 cup (75g) caster sugar

2 tablespoons Grand Marnier

1/2 teaspoon finely grated lemon rind

12 slices white bread

whisked custard

1 egg

1 egg white

2 tablespoons caster sugar

1/3 cup (80ml) skim milk

2 teaspoons arrowroot

1 teaspoon finely grated orange rind

Combine berries, sugar, liqueur and rind in large pan, stir gently over heat, without boiling, until sugar dissolves. Bring to boil; simmer, uncovered, without stirring, 5 minutes or until juices come out of berries. Strain berries and pour juice into shallow bowl.

Line four 1-cup (250ml) moulds with plastic wrap. Remove crusts from bread. Cut 4 rounds of bread to fit bases of moulds. Cut remaining 8 slices into 3 pieces each, taper slightly to fit around inside of moulds. Lightly dip 1 side of bread in berry juice; do not saturate bread. Line moulds with bread, coloured side down. Pieces should extend about 3cm above tops of moulds.

Using a slotted spoon, divide berry mixture between moulds, fold bread over to enclose. Pour remaining juices over puddings. Cover with plastic wrap, weight with a small can on each pudding, refrigerate overnight. Unmould, remove plastic wrap and serve with Whisked Custard.

Whisked Custard Combine all ingredients in medium heatproof bowl, whisk over pan of simmering water until custard is doubled in volume.

Per serve fat 3.6g; kJ 1588

cherries
jubilee

425g can seeded black cherries in syrup

1 tablespoon caster sugar

1 cinnamon stick

2 teaspoons arrowroot

1 tablespoon water

$1/3$ cup (80ml) brandy

1 litre low-fat vanilla ice-cream

Drain cherries, reserve syrup. Combine syrup, sugar and cinnamon stick in medium pan, bring to boil; simmer, uncovered, without stirring, 2 minutes. Strain; discard cinnamon stick.

Return syrup to pan, stir in blended arrowroot and water, stir over heat until sauce boils and thickens slightly. Add cherries, stir over low heat until warm.

Heat brandy, add to sauce, set aflame. Serve immediately with ice-cream.

Per serve fat 3.9g; kJ 1273

summer berry
clafoutis

cooking oil spray
200g boysenberries
200g blackberries
150g raspberries
100g blueberries
3 eggs
⅓ cup (75g) caster sugar
1 teaspoon vanilla essence
⅓ cup (50g) plain flour
1 tablespoon self-raising flour
¾ cup (180ml) skim milk

Coat four 1¾-cup (430ml) shallow ovenproof dishes with cooking oil spray; place on oven tray. Divide berries among dishes.

Whisk eggs, sugar and essence in medium bowl until frothy; whisk in sifted flours and milk, until just combined. Pour mixture, over back of spoon, into dishes.

Bake, uncovered, in moderate oven about 35 minutes or until clafoutis are set. Serve warm; dusted with sifted icing sugar, if desired.

Per serve fat 5.3g; kJ 1103

passionfruit pineapple
sorbet with mir

auce

You will need about 12 passionfruit for this recipe.

1 large (2kg) pineapple, peeled, cored, chopped

1/2 cup (110g) caster sugar

1 cup (250ml) water

1/2 cup (125ml) passionfruit pulp

3 egg whites

mint sauce

1/2 cup (125ml) passionfruit pulp

2/3 cup (160ml) water

2 tablespoons caster sugar

1/3 cup firmly packed fresh mint leaves

1/2 teaspoon arrowroot

1 teaspoon water, extra

Blend or process pineapple until smooth, push through a strainer; discard pulp. You will need 2 1/2 cups (625ml) juice.

Combine sugar and water in medium pan, stir over heat, without boiling, until sugar dissolves. Bring to boil; simmer, uncovered, without stirring, about 10 minutes, or until syrup is thick; set aside to cool.

Stir pineapple juice and passionfruit pulp into sugar syrup, pour into 20 x 30cm lamington pan, cover with foil, freeze until just firm.

Working quickly, process sorbet mixture and egg whites until smooth, pour into 14 x 21cm loaf pan, cover, freeze overnight. Serve with Mint Sauce.

Mint Sauce Push passionfruit pulp through coarse strainer, reserve juice and 1 teaspoon of the seeds. Combine reserved juice, water, sugar and mint in medium pan, stir over heat, without boiling, until sugar dissolves. Stir in blended arrowroot and extra water, simmer gently, stirring about 1 minute or until sauce is thickened slightly; strain. Stir in reserved seeds and chill.

Per serve fat 5.4g; kJ 1086

18 baked quinces
in orange syrup

3 large (1.2kg)
quinces

1 medium (180g)
orange

1¼ cups (275g) caster
sugar

1 cup (250ml) water

⅓ cup (80ml) orange
juice

½ teaspoon orange
flower water

Wipe quinces with damp cloth, prick skins all over with skewer. Wrap quinces individually in foil, stand upright, close together in ovenproof dish. Bake in moderately hot oven about 1 hour or until just tender.

Halve quinces, place cut side down in same baking dish.

Meanwhile, use a vegetable peeler to peel wide strips of rind thinly from orange. Combine rind, sugar, water, juice and orange flower water in small pan, stir over heat, without boiling, until sugar dissolves. Bring to boil; simmer, uncovered, without stirring, 5 minutes.

With a slotted spoon remove rind from syrup to wire rack over tray.

Pour syrup over quinces. Bake, uncovered, turning occasionally to coat with syrup, in moderately hot oven about 1 hour, or until quinces are soft and pink. Serve with rind and a spoonful of low-fat yogurt, if desired.

Per serve fat 0.4g;
kJ 1547

orange
souffles

cooking oil spray

1 tablespoon caster sugar

30g butter

1½ tablespoons plain flour

½ cup (125ml) skim milk

2 teaspoons finely grated orange rind

2 tablespoons orange juice

¼ cup (55g) caster sugar, extra

3 egg yolks

2 egg whites

Coat four ¾-cup (180ml) souffle dishes with cooking oil spray, sprinkle bases and sides with sugar, shake off excess. Place on oven tray.
Heat butter in medium pan, stir in flour; cook, stirring, until mixture thickens and bubbles. Gradually stir in combined milk, rind, juice and extra sugar, stir until mixture boils and thickens. Pour mixture into medium bowl, stir in egg yolks. Beat egg whites in small bowl with electric mixer until soft peaks form; fold gently into orange mixture in 2 batches.
Spoon into prepared dishes; level tops. Bake in moderately hot oven about 20 minutes or until souffles are puffed. Serve immediately; dusted with a little sifted icing sugar, if desired.

Per serve fat 11.2g; kJ 907

20 strawberry whip

¼ cup (55g) caster sugar
¾ cup (180ml) light evaporated milk, well chilled
3 teaspoons gelatine
¼ cup (60ml) water
250g strawberries

Combine sugar and ¼ cup (60ml) of the milk in small pan, stir over heat, without boiling, until sugar dissolves. Sprinkle gelatine over water in cup, stand in small pan of simmering water, stir until dissolved; stir into milk mixture.
Blend or process strawberries until smooth, stir into milk mixture. Transfer mixture to medium bowl; refrigerate until almost set.
Beat remaining milk in medium bowl with electric mixer until thick and creamy (do not overbeat). Beat strawberry mixture with electric mixer until thick and creamy, gently fold both mixtures together. Pour into 4 dessert glasses; refrigerate until set. Serve with extra strawberries, if desired; dusted with a little sifted icing sugar.

Per serve fat 0.7g; kJ 458

Sift flour and sugar into medium bowl; gradually whisk in combined egg oil and milk until smooth. Cover batter stand 30 minutes.

Pour 2 to 3 tablespoons of batte into heated heavy-based crepe pan which has been coated with cooking o spray; cook until lightly browned underneath. Turr crepe, lightly brown other side. Repeat with remaining batter. You will need 8 crepes for this recipe.

Divide Filling among crepes, fold into quarters; serve with Sauce and low-fat yogurt topped with toasted slivered almonds, if desired.

Filling Combine all ingredients in medium bowl, cover, refrigerate 2 hours. Drain, reserve liquid for Sauce.

Sauce Combine reserved liquid from Filling, brandy and juice in small pan, bring to boil; simmer, uncovered 2 minutes, cool before serving.

Per serve fat 3.9g; kJ 1254

3/4 cup (110g) plain flour

1 teaspoon caster sugar

1 egg, lightly beaten

1 teaspoon vegetable oil

1 1/3 cups (330ml) skim milk

cooking oil spray

filling

1 medium (200g) banana, sliced

200g blueberries

250g strawberries, quartered

1 teaspoon finely grated lemon rind

2 tablespoons golden syrup

sauce

2 tablespoons brandy

1/2 cup (125ml) orange juice

apple sponge

Peel, core, quarter and slice apples, combine in large pan with sugar and water; cook, covered, about 10 minutes or until apples are tender.

Spoon hot apple mixture into 1.5-litre (6-cup) deep 14cm round ovenproof dish; spread with Sponge Topping. Bake, uncovered, in moderate oven about 25 minutes. Serve drizzled with light cream, if desired.

Sponge Topping Beat eggs in small bowl with electric mixer about 7 minutes or until thick and creamy. Add sugar gradually, beating until dissolved between additions. Fold in sifted flours.

It is important to have the apple mixture as hot as possible before topping with the sponge mixture. The heat from the apples starts the cooking process.

4 large (800g) apples

¼ cup (55g) caster sugar

¼ cup (60ml) water

sponge topping

2 eggs

⅓ cup (75g) caster sugar

2 tablespoons cornflour

2 tablespoons plain flour

2 tablespoons self-raising flour

Per serve fat 2.9g; kJ 1267

2 large (240g) limes
3/4 cup (180ml) apple juice
3/4 cup (180ml) water
1/2 cup (110g) caster sugar
2 large (1.2kg) mangoes, sliced thickly
250g strawberries, halved
150g blueberries

spun toffee
3/4 cup (165g) caster sugar
1/4 cup (60ml) water

Using a vegetable peeler, peel rind thinly from limes, cut rind into very thin strips. Squeeze juice from limes; you will need 1/3 cup (80ml) of juice. Combine juices, water and sugar in medium heavy-based pan, stir over heat, without boiling, until sugar dissolves. Add rind, bring to boil; simmer, uncovered, without stirring, 15 minutes; cool. Place mango and berries on plates, pour over lime syrup; top with Spun Toffee.
Spun Toffee Combine sugar and water in small heavy-based pan, stir over heat, without boiling, until sugar dissolves. Bring to boil; boil, uncovered, without stirring, until toffee is golden brown. Cool about 5 minutes or until mixture is beginning to thicken. Dip 2 metal forks into toffee, pull forks apart to form thin strands of toffee. Place on plate until ready to serve.

Per serve fat 0.7g; kJ 2060

apple pinwheel

pudding

cooking oil spray

2½ cups (375g) self-raising flour

30g butter

¾ cup (180ml) skim milk,
approximately

2 tablespoons raspberry jam

2 medium (300g) apples, peeled,
grated

¾ cup (120g) chopped seeded
dates

½ teaspoon mixed spice

⅓ cup (80ml) boiling water

1 tablespoon golden syrup

Coat 1-litre (4-cup)
shallow ovenproof dish
with cooking oil spray.
Sift flour into large bowl, rub in
butter. Add enough milk to make a
soft dough. Knead dough gently on
floured surface until smooth.
Roll dough to 20 x 30cm rectangle.
Spread with jam; top with combined
apples, dates and spice; leaving a
3cm border along one long side.
Starting from opposite long side;
roll up tightly. Cut into 8 pieces.
Arrange pieces, cut side up, in
prepared dish. Pour over combined
water and golden syrup. Bake,
uncovered, in moderate oven about
40 minutes or until browned lightly
and cooked through.

Per serve fat 8.1g; kJ 2315

redcurrant sauce

4 medium (900g) firm ripe pears

1.5 litres (6 cups) water

8 rosehip tea bags

redcurrant sauce

½ cup (125ml) dry red wine

½ cup (125ml) redcurrant jelly

1½ tablespoons cornflour

Peel pears, leaving stems intact. Trim base of pears so they sit flat. Place pears in deep pan, add water and tea bags, bring to boil; simmer, covered, about 25 minutes or until pears are tender. Cool pears in liquid; reserve ¾ cup (180ml) of cooking liquid for sauce. Serve drained pears with Redcurrant Sauce and low-fat yogurt topped with toasted slivered almonds, if desired.

Redcurrant Sauce Combine wine, jelly, cornflour and reserved cooking liquid in medium pan, stir over heat until sauce boils and thickens; cool.

Per serve fat 0.2g; kJ 992

ream

We used an orange muscat. Any Sauternes style wine can be used.

1½ cups (375ml) muscat

½ cup (125ml) water

⅓ cup (80ml) orange juice

¼ cup (60ml) lime juice

¾ cup (165g) sugar

4 small (400g) carambola, sliced

6 (140g) fresh dates, seeded, halved

7 (140g) dried figs, halved

¾ cup (110g) dried apricots

2 cinnamon sticks

1 vanilla bean

5 cardamom pods, bruised

½ teaspoon finely grated lime rind

2 tablespoons shelled pistachios, chopped

ricotta cream

1 cup (200g) low-fat ricotta cheese

1½ tablespoons icing sugar mixture

¼ teaspoon ground cinnamon

1 tablespoon skim milk

Combine muscat, water, juices and sugar in large pan, stir over heat, without boiling, until sugar dissolves. Bring to boil; simmer, uncovered, without stirring, about 15 minutes or until syrup is thickened slightly.

Add carambola, dates, dried fruits, cinnamon, split vanilla bean, cardamom and rind to syrup. Simmer, uncovered, stirring occasionally, about 15 minutes or until fruit is tender. Cool syrup, cover, refrigerate 3 hours or overnight. Discard cinnamon sticks, vanilla bean and cardamom pods. Serve fruit mixture with Ricotta Cream and nuts.

Ricotta Cream Beat cheese, icing sugar and cinnamon in small bowl with electric mixer until smooth. Stir in milk.

Per serve fat 7.8g; kJ 2707

strawberry and watermelon
cocktail

*800g piece
watermelon*

*250g strawberries,
quartered*

*1 teaspoon finely
grated lemon rind*

*1 tablespoon lemon
juice*

*2 tablespoons dry
sherry*

*1/3 cup (75g) caster
sugar*

2/3 cup (160ml) water

Remove and discard skin from watermelon; cut
into 2cm cubes, removing seeds. Combine
melon and strawberries in large heatproof bowl.
Combine rind, juice, sherry, sugar and water in
medium pan, stir over heat, without boiling, until
sugar dissolves. Bring to boil; simmer,
uncovered, about 5 minutes or until thickened
slightly. Pour hot syrup over fruit in bowl. Cover,
refrigerate until cold.

Per serve fat 0.3g; kJ 525

lemon gelato
with sugared pastry twists

¹/₃ cup (80ml) water

³/₄ (165g) caster sugar

¹/₄ cup (60ml) light corn syrup

1¹/₂ cups (375ml) water, extra

1 tablespoon finely grated lemon rind

1¹/₂ cups (375ml) lemon juice

sugared pastry twists
¹/₂ sheet ready-rolled puff pastry

20g butter, melted

2 teaspoons cinnamon sugar

pinch ground clove

Combine water, sugar and corn syrup in small pan, stir over heat, without boiling, until sugar dissolves. Bring to boil; simmer uncovered, without stirring, 4 minutes. Stir in extra water, rind and juice; pour mixture into 20 x 30cm lamington pan, cover with foil, freeze until just firm. **Working** quickly, transfer gelato mixture to large bowl; beat with electric mixer until smooth. Return mixture to lamington pan, cover, freeze again until firm. Repeat process once more. Serve in scoops with Sugared Pastry Twists.

Sugared Pastry Twists Using a fluted pastry cutter, cut pastry widthways into 1cm strips. Brush with butter, sprinkle with combined cinnamon sugar and clove. Twist into decorative shapes, place on non-stick oven tray. Bake in moderate oven about 8 minutes or until lightly browned; cool on wire rack.

Per serve fat 5.4g; kJ 1086

biscotti

2 cups (300g) plain flour

2 eggs, lightly beaten

1 cup (220g) caster sugar

1/2 teaspoon grated orange rind

1/2 teaspoon vanilla essence

1/4 teaspoon baking powder

1/2 cup (75g) shelled pistachios, toasted

Sift flour into large bowl, add eggs, sugar, rind, essence and baking powder, mix to a smooth dough; mix in nuts.

Divide dough in half, roll each half on floured surface to 20cm sausage shape; place on greased oven tray. Bake in moderate oven about 30 minutes or until browned lightly and crusty; cool on trays.

Cut diagonally into 1.5cm slices, using a serrated knife. Place slices, cut side up, on greased oven trays. Bake in moderate oven about 25 minutes or until crisp; cool on wire racks before storing.

Makes about 26

Per serve fat 2g; kJ 396

rum balls

4 cups (400g) fine plain cake crumbs

1/4 cup (25g) cocoa

1/4 cup (60ml) apricot jam, warmed

2 tablespoons dark rum

2 tablespoons water

2/3 cup (70g) chocolate sprinkles

Combine crumbs and sifted cocoa in large bowl; stir in combined strained jam, rum and water. Roll 2 level teaspoons of mixture into balls. Roll balls in chocolate sprinkles. Refrigerate 2 hours before serving.

Makes about 45

Per serve fat 1.4g; kJ 286

Clockwise from top: coffee meringue twists, biscotti, rum balls, sugared jellies.

coffee meringue twists

1 egg white

1/3 cup (75g) caster sugar

1 teaspoon dry instant coffee

1 teaspoon hot water

Beat egg white in small bowl with electric mixer until soft peaks form. Gradually add sugar, beating until dissolved between additions. Stir in combined coffee and water.
Spoon mixture into piping bag fitted with small fluted tube. Pipe mixture into twists, about 5cm apart, on baking paper-covered oven trays. Bake in very slow oven about 1 hour or until meringues are firm to touch. Turn oven off, allow meringues to cool in oven.
Makes about 35
   Per serve fat 0g; kJ 36

sugared jellies

2 tablespoons gelatine

3/4 cup (180ml) water

2 cups (440g) caster sugar

3/4 cup (180ml) apple juice

1 tablespoon lemon juice

2 teaspoons grated lime rind

green food colouring

1/4 cup (55g) sugar

Line base and sides of 8 x 26cm bar pan with foil; grease foil.
Sprinkle gelatine over cold water in bowl, stand 5 minutes. Combine caster sugar and apple juice in pan, stir over heat, without boiling, until sugar dissolves; simmer, uncovered, without stirring, about 15 minutes or until temperature reaches 122°C on candy thermometer (a teaspoon of mixture will form a hard ball when dropped into a cup of cold water). Mixture must not change colour. Remove from heat, set aside to allow bubbles to subside.
Stir in gelatine mixture, lemon juice and rind. Tint mixture green with colouring, pour into prepared pan; cool. Refrigerate jelly until firm. Cut jelly into 2cm squares, place cubes onto wire rack, stand, uncovered, at least 12 hours. Toss jelly cubes in sugar.
Makes about 50
Per serve fat 0g; kJ 172

yogurt passionfruit
ice-cream

You will need about 3 passionfruit for this recipe.

1/4 cup (60ml) honey

400ml low-fat yogurt

2 teaspoons gelatine

1 tablespoon water

2 egg whites

1/4 cup (60ml) passionfruit pulp

Combine honey and yogurt in medium bowl. Sprinkle gelatine over water in cup, stand in small pan of simmering water, stir until dissolved; stir into yogurt mixture. Spread mixture into 20 x 30cm lamington pan, cover with foil, freeze until firm.

Chop yogurt mixture; beat in small bowl with electric mixer until mixture thickens and doubles in size, transfer to large bowl. Beat egg whites in clean small bowl with electric mixer until firm peaks form. Gently fold egg whites and passionfruit pulp into yogurt mixture. Pour into lamington pan, cover, freeze until firm.

Per serve fat 0.2g; kJ 580

You will need about 6 mandarins for this recipe.

³/₄ cup (110g) plain flour

3 eggs, lightly beaten

2 teaspoons vegetable oil

1 teaspoon finely grated mandarin rind

1 cup (250ml) skim milk

cooking oil spray

1 medium (200g) mandarin, segmented

mandarin syrup

1 tablespoon water

¹/₂ cup (110g) caster sugar

³/₄ cup (180ml) mandarin juice

1 tablespoon Grand Marnier

Sift flour into medium bowl, gradually whisk in combined eggs, oil, rind and milk until smooth. Cover batter, stand 30 minutes.

Pour 2 to 3 tablespoons of batter into heated heavy-based crepe pan which has been coated with cooking oil spray; cook until lightly browned underneath. Turn crepe, brown other side. Repeat with remaining batter. You will need 12 crepes for this recipe.

Divide mandarin segments among crepes, fold crepes into triangles; drizzle with Mandarin Syrup. Serve with low-fat yogurt, if desired.

Mandarin Syrup Combine water and sugar in medium pan, stir over heat, without boiling, until sugar dissolves.

Bring to boil; simmer, uncovered, without stirring, until syrup is golden brown. Remove from heat, stir in juice. Stir over heat until toffee is melted; stir in liqueur.

Per serve fat 7.6g; kJ 1487

plum and apple
cobbler

825g can dark plums in syrup

1 medium (150g) apple, sliced

½ teaspoon finely grated orange rind

2 tablespoons caster sugar

½ cup (75g) self-raising flour

¼ cup (35g) plain flour

2 tablespoons brown sugar

20g butter, chopped

1 egg, lightly beaten

2 tablespoons skim milk

¼ teaspoon ground cinnamon

Drain plums, reserve 2 tablespoons syrup. Halve plums, remove stones. Combine apple, rind, caster sugar and syrup in medium pan, bring to boil; simmer, covered, 8 minutes, stirring occasionally. Stir in plums, spoon into 1.5-litre (6-cup) ovenproof dish.

Sift flours into medium bowl, stir in brown sugar; rub in butter. Stir in egg and milk. Drop heaped tablespoons of mixture around edge of dish, sprinkle with cinnamon. Bake, uncovered, in moderate oven about 30 minutes or until browned.

Per serve fat 5.9g; kJ 1424

fresh berry
compote

250g strawberries

250g blackberries

250g raspberries

2 tablespoons caster sugar

$^1/_4$ cup (60ml) Grand Marnier

1 teaspoon finely grated orange rind

$1^1/_2$ cups (375ml) sparkling apple juice, well chilled

Combine berries, sugar, liqueur and rind in large bowl. Cover; refrigerate several hours, stirring occasionally.
Just before serving, spoon berries into 4 dessert glasses; pour over apple juice.

Per serve fat 0.3g; kJ 738

plum and apple strudel
with vanilla yogurt

2 large (400g) apples, peeled, cored

825g can dark plums in syrup, drained

2 teaspoons finely grated lemon rind

1/3 cup (75g) firmly packed brown sugar

1/4 cup (60ml) maple-flavoured syrup

1/4 cup (60ml) water

1 cinnamon stick

1/2 cup (60g) almond meal

6 sheets fillo pastry

cooking oil spray

vanilla yogurt

1/3 cup (80ml) skim milk

3/4 cup (180ml) low-fat yogurt

2 teaspoons vanilla essence

1/4 cup (40g) icing sugar mixture

Cut each apple into 12 pieces. Halve plums, discard stones. Combine apple, rind, sugar, maple syrup, water and cinnamon in large pan, stir over heat, without boiling, until sugar dissolves. Bring to boil; simmer, uncovered, 10 minutes or until apple is just tender, stirring occasionally. Drain apple mixture, discard cinnamon and syrup; cool. Combine apple, plums and almond meal in bowl; mix gently.

Layer pastry sheets together, coating every second sheet with cooking oil spray. Spoon apple mixture along long edge of pastry, leaving 8cm border at each end. Roll up strudel, tucking in ends while rolling; coat lightly with cooking oil spray.

Place strudel on oven tray which has been coated with cooking oil spray, bake, uncovered, in moderate oven about 30 minutes or until browned. Serve dusted with sifted icing sugar and candied lemon rind, if desired. Serve with Vanilla Yogurt.

Vanilla Yogurt Combine all ingredients in medium bowl.

Per serve fat 9.6g; kJ 1959

42 rice pudding

with sultanas

cooking oil spray

½ cup (100g) white short-grain rice

2½ cups (625ml) skim milk

¼ cup (55g) caster sugar

2 tablespoons sultanas

1 teaspoon vanilla essence

2 teaspoons soft butter

grated nutmeg

Coat 1-litre (4-cup) shallow ovenproof dish with cooking oil spray. Wash rice well under cold water; drain.

Combine rice, milk, sugar, sultanas and essence in prepared dish, mix lightly with a fork. Top with butter, sprinkle with nutmeg.

Bake, uncovered, in moderately slow oven about 2 hours or until most of the milk has been absorbed. Serve warm or cold with fresh or poached fruit, if desired.

Per serve fat 5.1g; kJ 1091

buttermilk

pancakes with golden pears

1 cup (150g) self-raising flour

1 cup (250ml) buttermilk

1/4 cup (60ml) skim milk

1 egg white

cooking oil spray

golden pears

2 medium (460g) pears, halved

1/4 cup (60ml) golden syrup

1 cup (250ml) water

1 tablespoon lemon juice

3 teaspoons cornflour

1 tablespoon water, extra

Sift flour into medium bowl, gradually whisk in combined milks until smooth. Beat egg white in small bowl with electric mixer until soft peaks form, fold gently into batter. **Pour** 1/2 cup (125ml) of batter into heated non-stick pan which has been coated with cooking oil spray; cook about 2 minutes or until browned underneath. Turn pancake, brown other side. Repeat with remaining batter. You will need 4 pancakes for this recipe. Serve pancakes with Golden Pears and syrup.

Golden Pears Place pears in medium pan with golden syrup, water and juice, bring to boil; simmer, uncovered, until pears are just tender.

Remove pears from syrup; reserve syrup. Slice pears lengthways. Stir blended cornflour and extra water into reserved syrup in pan, stir over heat until syrup boils and thickens slightly.

Per serve fat 2.6g; kJ 1271

¾ cup (150g) low-fat ricotta cheese, sieved

1 tablespoon finely grated orange rind

1 teaspoon ground cinnamon

1 egg yolk

1 tablespoon caster sugar

4 sheets fillo pastry

cooking oil spray

rhubarb topping

5 cups (550g) chopped fresh rhubarb

½ small (65g) apple, peeled, chopped

1 teaspoon finely grated fresh ginger

⅓ cup (75g) caster sugar

Combine cheese, rind, cinnamon, egg yolk and sugar in medium bowl.

Cut pastry sheets in half; layer pastry sheets together, coating every second sheet with cooking oil spray. Cut 24cm round from layered pastry; cut decorative shapes from pastry scraps, if desired. Place pastry round on oven tray which has been coated with cooking oil spray; spread cheese mixture evenly over base, leaving 3cm border. Bake, uncovered, in moderate oven about 20 minutes or until cheese mixture is set.

Spread Rhubarb Topping over base; decorate with pastry shapes. Bake, uncovered, in moderate oven about 25 minutes or until firm. Serve dusted with a little sifted icing sugar, if desired.

Rhubarb Topping Combine rhubarb, apple, ginger and sugar in large pan, stir over heat, until sugar dissolves. Cook, uncovered, stirring occasionally, about 15 minutes or until mixture is thick.

Per serve fat 6.1g; kJ 1020

fruit and yogurt
crepes

1/4 cup (35g) plain flour

1/4 cup (40g) wholemeal plain flour

1 teaspoon caster sugar

1 egg, lightly beaten

3/4 cup (180ml) skim milk

2 teaspoons vegetable oil

1 teaspoon finely grated lemon rind

cooking oil spray

2 medium (400g) peaches

250g strawberries

spiced yogurt

1½ cups (375ml) low-fat yogurt

1½ tablespoons brown sugar

1 teaspoon finely grated lemon rind

½ teaspoon ground cinnamon

Sift flours and sugar into medium bowl, gradually whisk in combined egg, milk, oil and rind until smooth. Cover batter; refrigerate 30 minutes.

Pour 2 to 3 tablespoons of batter into heated heavy-based crepe pan which has been coated with cooking oil spray; cook until lightly browned underneath. Turn crepe, brown other side. Repeat with remaining batter.

Peel and slice peaches; cut strawberries into wedges. Divide fruit among crepes; fold crepes over fruit. Serve with Spiced yogurt.

Spiced yogurt Combine all ingredients in bowl; stir until smooth.

Per serve fat 5.3g; kJ 1002

banana and carob chip

ice-cream

You will need about 2 large (460g) over-ripe bananas for this recipe.

1 cup (250ml) light evaporated milk

1 cup mashed banana

¹/₂ cup (125ml) low-fat yogurt

¹/₄ cup (60ml) skim milk

¹/₄ cup (60ml) maple-flavoured syrup

2 teaspoons vanilla essence

¹/₃ cup (55g) carob buttons, chopped

Pour evaporated milk into 14 x 21cm loaf pan, cover with foil, freeze until just firm. Process evaporated milk, banana, yogurt, skim milk, maple syrup and essence until thick and creamy. Pour mixture into loaf pan, cover, freeze until just firm. Repeat processing, stir in carob, cover, freeze until firm.

Per serve fat 3.8g; kJ 997

48 banana
souffles

You will need about 1 medium (200g) over-ripe banana for this recipe.

cooking oil spray

2¹/₂ tablespoons caster sugar

2 tablespoons cornflour

¹/₄ cup mashed banana

2 egg yolks

¹/₂ cup (125ml) skim milk

6 egg whites

2 tablespoons caster sugar, extra

Coat four 1¹/₄-cup (310ml) souffle dishes with cooking oil spray; sprinkle bases and sides with 1 tablespoon of the sugar, shake off excess.
Whisk remaining 1¹/₂ tablespoons of sugar, cornflour, banana and egg yolks in large bowl until combined. Bring milk to boil in medium pan; gradually whisk hot milk into banana mixture. Return mixture to pan; whisk over heat until banana mixture boils and becomes very thick. Transfer banana mixture to large bowl, cover surface with plastic wrap; cool 5 minutes.
Beat egg whites in medium bowl with electric mixer until soft peaks form, gradually add extra sugar, beating until firm peaks form. Gently fold egg white mixture into banana mixture in 2 batches. Spoon mixture into prepared dishes; smooth tops. Place a thin slice of banana on each souffle, if desired. Bake in moderately hot oven about 20 minutes or until souffles are puffed. Serve immediately; dusted with a little sifted icing sugar, if desired.

Per serve fat 3.7g; kJ 823

ricotta
pancakes

1 cup (150g) white self-raising flour

1 cup (160g) wholemeal self-raising flour

1/3 cup (75g) caster sugar

1 cup (200g) low-fat ricotta cheese

1 1/2 cups (375ml) skim milk

2 egg whites

cooking oil spray

1/2 cup (125ml) maple-flavoured syrup

1 litre low-fat vanilla ice-cream

Sift flours and sugar into large bowl, whisk in cheese and milk. Beat egg whites in small bowl with electric mixer until soft peaks form, fold into ricotta mixture.

Drop 1/2 cup (125ml) of batter into heated non-stick pan which has been coated with cooking oil spray, spread to 14cm round; cook about 2 minutes or until browned underneath. Turn pancake, brown other side. Repeat with remaining batter. You will need 8 pancakes for this recipe.

Serve pancakes with maple syrup and ice-cream; top with fresh berries, if desired.

Per serve fat 10.2g; kJ 2871

crepes with
vanilla cream and raspberries

3/4 cup (110g) plain flour
1 tablespoon caster sugar
1/2 teaspoon ground ginger
1 egg
1 1/4 cups (310ml) skim milk
cooking oil spray
100g raspberries

vanilla cream
50g packaged low-fat cream cheese
2 tablespoons sour light cream
2 teaspoons icing sugar mixture
1 teaspoon vanilla essence

Sift flour, sugar and ginger into medium bowl, gradually whisk in combined egg and milk until smooth. Cover batter, stand 30 minutes.
Pour 1/4 cup (60ml) of batter into heated heavy-based crepe pan which has been coated with cooking oil spray; cook until lightly browned underneath. Turn crepe, brown other side. Repeat with remaining batter. You will need 8 crepes for this recipe. Serve crepes with Vanilla Cream and raspberries.
Vanilla Cream Combine all ingredients in bowl.

Per serve fat 8.8g; kJ 1063

52 spicy baked apples

4 medium (600g) apples

20g soft butter

¼ cup (50g) brown sugar

2 teaspoons rosewater

½ teaspoon ground cinnamon

pinch ground cardamom

1 tablespoon pine nuts, toasted

2 tablespoons shelled pistachios, toasted, chopped

¼ cup (35g) dried currants

1 tablespoon chopped dried apricots

1 tablespoon chopped dried figs

honey fromage frais

2 teaspoons rosewater

200g low-fat vanilla fromage frais

2 teaspoons honey

Remove cores and slit skin of each apple around centre. Cut shallow 3cm hole in top of each apple. Combine remaining ingredients in small bowl. Spoon mixture into apple cavities.
Place apples in large ovenproof dish; bake, covered, in moderately hot oven about 35 minutes or until apples are tender. Serve with pan juices and Honey Fromage Frais.
Honey Fromage Frais Combine all ingredients in small bowl.

Per serve fat 12.9g; kJ 1195

boysenberry apple
crumble

200g boysenberries
1 large (200g) apple, chopped
3 teaspoons caster sugar

topping
1/3 cup (35g) natural muesli
1 tablespoon plain flour
2 teaspoons brown sugar
30g butter

Combine berries, apple and sugar in medium pan; simmer, uncovered, until apple is just tender. Divide berry mixture among four 3/4-cup (180ml) ovenproof dishes; sprinkle with Topping.

Bake, uncovered, in moderate oven about 15 minutes or until browned.

Topping Combine muesli, flour and brown sugar in medium bowl; rub in butter.

Per serve fat 7g; kJ 652

54 rich chocolate

self-saucing pudding

cooking oil spray

1 cup (150g) self-raising flour

³/₄ cup (165g) caster sugar

2 tablespoons cocoa powder

¹/₂ cup (125ml) skim milk

1 teaspoon vanilla essence

30g butter, melted

³/₄ cup (150g) firmly packed brown sugar

¹/₄ cup (25g) cocoa powder, extra

1³/₄ cups (430ml) hot water

Coat 2-litre (8-cup) ovenproof dish with cooking oil spray. **Sift** flour, caster sugar and cocoa into large bowl; add combined milk, essence and butter, stir until smooth. Pour mixture into prepared dish; sift combined brown sugar and extra cocoa evenly over top. **Carefully** pour hot water over pudding. Bake, uncovered, in moderate oven about 50 minutes or until pudding is firm. Serve dusted with sifted icing sugar, if desired.

Per serve fat 8.8g; kJ 2208

56 strawberries and passionfruit with meringue

You will need about 3 passionfruit for this recipe.

500g strawberries, halved

2 egg whites

1/3 cup (75g) caster sugar

passionfruit sauce

1/2 cup (125ml) water

1/4 cup (60ml) passionfruit pulp

2 tablespoons caster sugar

3 teaspoons cornflour

Pour Passionfruit Sauce onto four heatproof plates. Arrange strawberries in a single layer on top of sauce.

Beat egg whites in small bowl with electric mixer until soft peaks form, gradually add sugar, beating until dissolved between additions. Spoon meringue mixture over strawberries; grill until meringue is browned lightly.

Passionfruit Sauce Combine all ingredients in small pan, stir over heat until sauce boils and thickens. **Strain** sauce; return a few of the seeds to sauce.

Per serve fat 0.1g; kJ 642

125g strawberries, sliced

1 tablespoon water

1 tablespoon caster sugar

425g can sliced peaches in natural juice

2 tablespoons brandy

4 (70g) frozen waffles

½ cup (125ml) low-fat yogurt

1 tablespoon chopped shelled pistachios

Combine strawberries, water and sugar in medium pan, bring to boil; simmer, covered, 5 minutes or until strawberries are soft. Blend or process strawberry mixture until thick and smooth.

Drain peaches, reserve ½ cup (125ml) juice. Combine peaches, brandy and reserved juice in bowl.

Toast waffles, serve with peach mixture, yogurt and strawberry sauce; sprinkle with nuts.

Per serve fat 3g; kJ 728

58 date syrup
pancakes

1 1/2 cups (225g) self-raising flour

1/2 cup (75g) plain flour

1/2 teaspoon ground cardamom

1/2 teaspoon mixed spice

1 tablespoon brown sugar

1 egg, lightly beaten

1 1/4 cups (310ml) skim milk,
approximately

cooking oil spray

date syrup

1 medium (75g) lime

3 cups (660g) caster sugar

2 cups (500ml) water

3 cardamom pods, bruised

1 cinnamon stick

10 (230g) fresh dates, seeded,
sliced

Sift flours and spices into large bowl, stir in sugar. Gradually stir in egg and enough milk to form a thick batter. Cover batter, refrigerate 30 minutes.

Drop 1/4 cup (60ml) of batter into heated heavy-based pan which has been coated with cooking oil spray. Spread to 10cm round; cook about 2 minutes or until browned underneath. Turn pancake, brown other side. Repeat with remaining batter. Place pancakes onto plate; pour over hot Date Syrup.

Date Syrup Using vegetable peeler, peel strips of rind from half the lime, cut rind into very thin strips.

Combine sugar and water in medium pan, stir over heat, without boiling, until sugar dissolves. Add lime rind, cardamom and cinnamon. Bring to boil; simmer, uncovered, without stirring, 3 minutes. Add dates; simmer, uncovered, 3 minutes or until mixture is thickened slightly. Discard cinnamon stick.

Per serve fat 3g; kJ 4165

glossary

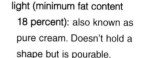

almond kernels natural kernels with skins.

almond meal blanched ground almonds.

amaretto almond-flavoured liqueur.

angostura aromatic bitters based on rum, infused with bitter aromatic bark, herbs and spices.

arrowroot used mostly for thickening. Cornflour can be substituted but will not give as clear a glaze.

baking powder a raising agent consisting mainly of 2 parts cream of tartar to 1 part bicarbonate of soda (baking soda).

breadcrumbs

stale: one- or two-day-old bread made into crumbs by grating, blending or processing.

carambola also known as star fruit; five-cornered, pale golden-yellow, crisp and juicy fruit with a waxy edible skin.

carob buttons chocolate substitute; available from health food stores.

cheese

light cream: the version of Philadelphia cream cheese with 30 percent less fat.

low-fat ricotta: a low-fat, fresh, unripened cheese made from whey.

cocoa cocoa powder.

cornflour also known as cornstarch.

corn syrup available in light or dark colour; glucose syrup (liquid glucose) can be substituted.

cream

low-fat sour (minimum fat content 18 percent): a less dense, commercially cultured soured cream.

light (minimum fat content 18 percent): also known as pure cream. Doesn't hold a shape but is pourable.

essence extract.

flour

white plain: an all-purpose flour, made from wheat.

white self-raising: plain flour sifted with baking powder in the proportion of 1 cup flour to 2 teaspoons baking powder.

wholemeal plain: also known as all-purpose wholewheat flour, has no baking powder added.

wholemeal self-raising: wholewheat self-raising flour; add baking powder as above to make wholemeal self-raising flour.

fromage frais we used fruche light with 0.5 percent fat content; available from supermarkets.

gelatine (gelatin) we used powdered gelatine. It is also available in sheet form known as leaf gelatine.

glucose syrup also known as liquid glucose; a sugary syrup obtained from starches such as wheat and corn. Prevents sugar crystallisation when used in making confectionery.

golden syrup a by-product of refined sugar cane; pure maple syrup or honey can be substituted.

grand marnier orange-flavoured liqueur based on cognac.

ice-cream, vanilla, low fat we used an ice-cream with a 3 percent fat content.

jam also known as preserve or conserve; most often made from fruit.

kiwi fruit also known as Chinese gooseberry.

la grande passion armagnac and passionfruit-flavoured liqueur.

maple-flavoured syrup also known as pancake syrup; not a substitute for pure maple syrup.

milk

buttermilk: low-fat milk cultured to give a slightly sour, tangy taste.

evaporated, light: canned milk with 0.3 percent fat .

skim: we used milk with 0.1 percent fat content.

mixed spice a blend of ground spices usually consisting of cinnamon, allspice and nutmeg.

muscat a sweet, musky flavoured fortified wine; made from muscat grapes.

oil

cooking-oil spray: vegetable oil in an aerosol can, available in supermarkets.

vegetable: any of a number of oils sourced from plants rather than animal fats.

orange flower water concentrated flavouring made from orange blossoms.

pawpaw also known as papaya or papaw; large, pear-shaped red-orange tropical fruit. Sometimes use unripe (green) in cooking.

pernod an aniseed-flavoured liqueur.

rosewater extract made from crushed rose petals, called gulab in India; used for its aromatic quality in many sweetmeats and desserts.

rum, dark we prefer to use an underproof rum for a more subtle flavour.

saffron stigma of a member of the crocus family, available in strands or ground form; imparts a yellow-orange colour to food once infused. Quality varies greatly. Should be stored in the freezer.

star anise a dried star-shaped pod whose seeds have an astringent aniseed flavour.

sugar we used coarse, granulated table sugar, also known as crystal sugar, unless otherwise specified.

brown: an extremely soft, fine granulated sugar retaining molasses for its characteristic colour and flavour.

caster: also known as superfine or finely granulated table sugar.

cinnamon sugar: combination of ground cinnamon and caster sugar.

icing sugar mixture: also known as confectioners' sugar or powdered sugar; granulated sugar crushed together with a small amount (about 3 percent) cornflour added.

pure icing: also known as confectioners' sugar.

sultanas golden raisins.

yogurt

low-fat plain: we used yogurt with a fat content of less than 0.2 percent.

low-fat vanilla: we used a vanilla flavoured yogurt with a fat content of 0.1 percent.

62

index

facts and figures 63

These conversions are approximate only, but the difference between an exact and the approximate conversion of various liquid and dry measures is minimal and will not affect your cooking results.

Measuring equipment

The difference between one country's measuring cups and another's is, at most, within a 2 or 3 teaspoon variance. (For the record, 1 Australian metric measuring cup holds approximately 250ml.) The most accurate way of measuring dry ingredients is to weigh them. For liquids, use a clear glass or plastic jug having metric markings.

Note: NZ, Canada, USA and UK all use 15ml tablespoons. Australian tablespoons measure 20ml.
All cup and spoon measurements are level.

How to measure

When using graduated measuring cups, shake dry ingredients loosely into the appropriate cup. Do not tap the cup on a bench or tightly pack the ingredients unless directed to do so. Level the top of measuring cups and measuring spoons with a knife. When measuring liquids, place a clear glass or plastic jug having metric markings on a flat surface to check accuracy at eye level.

Dry Measures

metric	imperial
15g	1/2oz
30g	1oz
60g	2oz
90g	3oz
125g	4oz (1/4lb)
155g	5oz
185g	6oz
220g	7oz
250g	8oz (1/2lb)
280g	9oz
315g	10oz
345g	11oz
375g	12oz (3/4lb)
410g	13oz
440g	14oz
470g	15oz
500g	16oz (1lb)
750g	24oz (11/2lb)
1kg	32oz (2lb)

We use large eggs having an average weight of 60g.

Liquid Measures

metric	imperial
30ml	1 fluid oz
60ml	2 fluid oz
100ml	3 fluid oz
125ml	4 fluid oz
150ml	5 fluid oz (1/4 pint/1 gill)
190ml	6 fluid oz
250ml (1cup)	8 fluid oz
300ml	10 fluid oz (1/2 pint)
500ml	16 fluid oz
600ml	20 fluid oz (1 pint)
1000ml (1litre)	13/4 pints

Helpful Measures

metric	imperial
3mm	1/8in
6mm	1/4in
1cm	1/2in
2cm	3/4in
2.5cm	1in
6cm	21/2in
8cm	3in
20cm	8in
23cm	9in
25cm	10in
30cm	12in (1ft)

Oven Temperatures

These oven temperatures are only a guide. Always check the manufacturer's manual.

	C°(Celsius)	F°(Fahrenheit)	Gas Mark
Very slow	120	250	1
Slow	150	300	2
Moderately slow	160	325	3
Moderate	180 –190	350 – 375	4
Moderately hot	200 – 210	400 – 425	5
Hot	220 – 230	450 – 475	6
Very hot	240 – 250	500 – 525	7

Food editor Pamela Clark
Associate food editor Karen Hammial
Assistant food editor Kathy McGarry
Assistant recipe editor Elizabeth Hooper
Home Library Staff
Editor-in-chief Mary Coleman
Marketing manager Nicole Pizanis
Editor Susan Tomnay
Subeditor Bianca Martin
Concept design Jackie Richards
Designer Sue de Guingand
Group publisher Paul Dykzeul

Produced by *The Australian Women's Weekly* Home Library, Sydney.
Colour separations by ACP Colour Graphics Pty Ltd, Sydney.
Printing by Diamond Press Limited, Sydney.
Published by ACP Publishing Pty Limited, 54 Park St, Sydney;
GPO Box 4088, Sydney, NSW 1028. Ph: (02) 9282 8618 Fax: (02) 9267 9438.
AWWHomeLib@publishing.acp.com.au
Australia: Distributed by Network Distribution Company,
GPO Box 4088, Sydney, NSW 1028. Ph: (02) 9282 8777 Fax: (02) 9264 3278.
United Kingdom: Distributed by Australian Consolidated Press (UK),
Moulton Park Business Centre, Red House Rd, Moulton Park, Northampton, NN3 6AQ.
Ph: (01604) 497 531 Fax: (01604) 497 533 Acpukltd@aol.com
Canada: Distributed by Whitecap Books Ltd,
351 Lynn Ave, North Vancouver, BC, V7J 2C4, (604) 980 9852.
New Zealand: Distributed by Netlink Distribution Company,
17B Hargreaves St, Level 5, College Hill, Auckland 1, (9) 302 7616.
South Africa: Distributed by PSD Promotions (Pty) Ltd,
PO Box 1175, Isando 1600, SA, (011) 392 6065.
Sweet and Simple: Healthy Desserts
Includes index.
ISBN 1 86396 126 7.
1Cookery (Puddings). 2. Desserts. I Title: Australian Women's Weekly.
(Series: Australian Women's Weekly sweet and simple mini series).
641.86
ACP Publishing Pty Limited 1999
ACN 053 273 546

Cover: Fruit and yogurt crepes, page 46.
Photographer Scott Cameron
Back cover: Lemon gelato with sugared pastry twists, page 31.